The EFT Workbook For Confidence

Suzanne Zacharia

DEDICATION

This book is dedicated to all who want to reach their full potential.

CONTENTS

ACKNOWLEDGMENTS

I would like to thank Kelly Haynes, Sharon Gordon, Geraldine Davies, and Michelle Elaawar, practitioners who worked with me at the very first clinic which was all my own. It is through their feedback and initially with them in mind that this book was first developed. Michelle also is my daughter, and I thank her for pushing me to get this book published in its present format.

And of course, many thanks are due to Gary Craig, the founder of EFT, without whom this progress in the history of mankind would not have been possible.

Last but by no means least, I thank all my lovely clients and Level 3 EFT trainees who have given their feedback and encouragement, which helped develop this book.

1   WHAT IS EFT?

EFT is known to some as "Energy Psychology" and others as "Tapping" method. It is used by many as a self-help method for any emotional or physical condition. EFT and other forms of Tapping are also very popular with modern advanced hypnotists, who are discovering just how easy this new method is to add to their repertoire.

Indeed, EFT is fast replacing hypnosis as the number 1 popular method to blast through blocks to your confidence.

You may be new to EFT, or it may be a familiar friend already. Either way, you can learn EFT very easily from the versions in this manual.

You may even be an experienced EFT practitioner; some of the best are amongst my readers.

EFT works on the principle that what causes undesirable feelings and behavior is a disruption in the body's energy system.

This energy is the same energy that various therapies and self-help modalities talk about, including acupuncture, Reiki, Yoga, and Shiatsu.

In essence, when we do EFT, we:
- Remove the "wrong" energy from our body by using the meridian lines as a kind of waste disposal system.
- Access this "wrong" energy to be removed by calling it up.

So when we do EFT, we:
- Tap on important points in the body's meridian system.
- Call up the waste energy to be disposed of by saying a Reminder phrase.

This is like:

- Your waste disposal people come to collect your household waste.
- In order for them to do so, you pick it up and put it out for them to collect.

It is important to understand that in EFT we only briefly connect to the negative. We safely and gently dispose of it. And to dispose of it, we need to safely collect it and throw it away.

This is so effective that sometimes, people forget they ever had a problem with something in the first place. That's OK, I don't mind how you achieved freedom using this book, just that you did! If you are a practitioner, no doubt you feel the same. This is all about long-lasting efficient results.

2   OK, NOW LET'S DO EFT!

There is a simple and easy-to-follow version of EFT used in this manual. If you know EFT already, great. If not, you will find it easy to follow from the illustrations in this book. If you would like to see an EFT demonstration in action, you can go to my website and run the easy instructional video clip on the EFT With Me page here:

www.EFT-Scripts.com

You can be an accomplished EFTer very soon!

<u>Important Notice:</u>

- You must assume responsibility for your own physical and mental wellbeing and not do anything that is not right for you. For example, if you are now diagnosed with schizophrenia or psychosis, EFT is unlikely to be suitable for you.
- Regardless of the above proviso, you are advised to consult with your physician or medical practitioner before embarking on any alternative or complementary treatment.
- This book is not a substitute for medical advice and care, nor was it intended to be.
- A very small minority of people, about 1%, have what is called an energy toxin. This stops EFT from working. You can only tell if none of the exercises in here whatsoever lead to any reduction in SUDS, or numbers. If one exercise does and another does not, you do not have an energy toxin.
- A very small minority again of readers may have a multitude of unresolved issues from a harrowing childhood. If that is the case, I strongly advise you to work with an experienced practitioner.

I will explain to you all the points you need to use. Then we will do a dummy run. And then we will start the EFT process towards your freedom from lack of confidence.

We start each round of tapping with a Setup phrase said 3 times, unless otherwise specified. We continue the round saying a Reminder phrase. A round of EFT is a sequence of EFT going around the body once.

You can use one hand or the other for tapping. Some, like me, prefer to use both hands at once. It does not matter to the results and is a matter of personal choice.

We tap with at least two fingers and preferably more. If you have nice long nails, just tap with the pads of your fingers to avoid bruising yourself with your nails. The EFT acupressure points we are going to use are listed below and illustrated overleaf.

For the Setup phrase
- The Karate Chop (the hitting edge of your hand if playing Karate)

For the Reminder phrase
- Top of the Head (where you have a swirly thing at the crown)
- Eye Brow (where the eyebrow usually meets the top of the nose)
- Side of the Eye (where your eyebrow ends)
- Under the Eye (on your cheekbone)
- Under the Nose (between your nose and mouth)
- Chin (in the middle of the horizontal line on your chin)
- The mis-named Collarbone (on the bony protrusion just either side of the "V" at the bottom of your neck)
- Under the Arm (under your arm where if you were female and wearing a bra, it would be the middle of the bra strap on the side of your body)

We tap on each point with at least two fingers. This way, we do not have to find the exact spot. We tap all the while we are saying our statements, as if tapping in time to music.

If you have a disability that precludes you from reaching some of the points or tapping with two fingers, do not worry about it! EFT is a very robust system.

You can leave some points out and it still works.

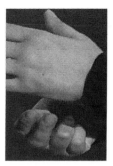

Tapping on the Karate Chop
(the hitting edge of your hand if playing Karate)
We say the Setup statement **3 times** as we tap continuously on the
Karate Chop. And in this book, you do it 3 times unless directed
otherwise. If in doubt, do it 3 times anyway. If you cannot use the Karate
Chop (for example, in case of extreme eczema on that area), simply use
any of the other points instead for the Setup, and still say it 3 times.

Top of the Head
(where you have a swirly thing at the crown)

Eye Brow
(where the eyebrow usually meets the top of the nose)

Side of the Eye (on the bone, kind of where your eyebrow ends)

Under the Eye (on your cheekbone, just over 2 cm under your pupil)

Under the Nose (between your nose and mouth)

Chin (in the middle of the horizontal line on your chin)

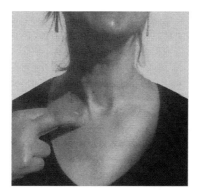

The mis-named Collarbone (on the bony protrusion just either side of the "V" at the bottom of your neck)

Under the Arm (under your arm where if a woman is wearing a bra, it would be the middle of the bra strap on the side of the body)

Now let's do a "practice run" so that you will be familiar with the tapping procedure. And Remember...

It may feel strange at first and ALL new things seem strange at first.

The reason why EFT is taking the world by storm is just that it is such an effective self-help tool. I don't know with 100% certainty that it will work with you, but since it has helped so many of my clients, chances are that you will soon be speaking very highly of it too.

"Do not fear to be eccentric in opinion, for every opinion now accepted was once eccentric" (Bertrand Russell)

When/if you are already familiar with the points, just follow the tapping instructions on the next page. It's easy!

If you are an experienced EFTer tapping for your own confidence freedom, or for ideas on how to conduct sessions as an already fully-qualified EFT Practitioner, you may prefer to skip the next chapter or two.

Now for your practice run...

Tap on the Karate Chop continuously as you say this Setup statement **three times**.

Setup
"Even though I'm doing this silly tapping thing, I accept myself, and that's OK, even if I don't"

Now tap on the Top of the Head continuously as you say this Reminder statement **once.**

Reminder
"This silly tapping thing"

Now tap on the Eye Brow continuously as you say this Reminder statement **once**.

Reminder
"This silly tapping thing"

Next tap on the Side of Eye continuously as you say this Reminder statement **once**.

Reminder
"This silly tapping thing"

Now tap on the Under Eye continuously as you say this Reminder statement **once.**

Reminder
"This silly tapping thing"

Next tap on the Under Nose point continuously as you say this Reminder statement **once**.

Reminder
"This silly tapping thing"

Tap on the Chin continuously as you say this Reminder statement **once**.

Reminder
"This silly tapping thing"

And now tap on the Collarbone continuously as you say this Reminder statement **once**.
Reminder
"This silly tapping thing"

Next tap on the Under Arm continuously as you say this Reminder statement **once**.

Reminder
"This silly tapping thing"

And that's it!

You may wonder what this has to do with confidence. Well, let me put it this way. I used to be terrified when speaking to people in authority.

Compared to that, tapping on top of my head was far less silly!

And I am pleased to assure you the results have lasted to this day too. No more tapping needed for it either.

3 SUDS OR LEVEL OF NEGATIVE FEELINGS

SUDS is a term for the Subjective Unit of Distress Scale, or how upset we could feel. We will be measuring the level of fear, stress, or any negative emotions in various situations. This can be nervousness, fear, shame, sadness, anger, guilt, or any negative emotions felt. You do not need to identify what the feeling exactly is, just get an idea of how intense it is. This is so that you can tell when it is gone and move onto the next step.

- If these are past or future situations, then imagine how intense you would feel if you were to think about these situations.

- If these are in the present moment, simply have a guess at the intensity of negative feeling you experience.

Each situation you tap for has to be **specific**. The more specific you can be (EG "When visiting my friend Amy", or "the day my colleague shouted at me"), the better.

We measure the SUDS from 10 to 0, 10 being the worst, 0 being neutral or nothing. We aim to get all SUDS to 0 for complete success.

For non-practitioners, SUDS sometimes present a challenge. Typically, if you are working on yourself you may be unsure about the SUDS themselves. If this is the case, that is **OK**. Just rate the intensity of feeling Small, Medium, or Large. Or you can rate it Present or Absent. Simple.

If after tapping several rounds of EFT, there is no intensity, that is OK too. It probably means zero. It is not an exact science. There is no need to get yourself all worked up about "doing it right". EFT is very robust. This book is all about getting **results**, not a judgment of how you are doing the technique!

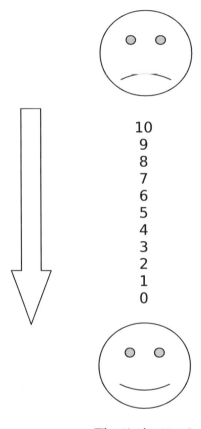

That's better!

Remember, this book is not about doing EFT exactly right, it is simply about losing the lack of confidence. As long as you lose the lack of confidence, that's all that matters.

Sometimes, instead of the numbers going down, they go up. This can be understandably scary at first. But it shows that there is a **very relevant issue uncovered** that lies underneath the issue being worked on. If that happens, one of the following steps can help

☐   Say the Setup statement with gusto, and follow it by shouting (in your mind if need be) "I DEEPLY ACCEPT MYSELF". Even if you do not really believe it, that's OK. You do not have to believe what you say for EFT to work. Then tap again and see how the numbers go this time.

- Drink water. EFT requires water. If you are doing this for a fear of swallowing, you can wet your tongue with water, it will help.
- Get up and stretch. This helps move stagnant energy.
- Simply ask yourself: "If there was a specific person or specific event that this reminds me of, what would it be?" Then work on whatever comes up.

Remember, there is no need to get yourself all worked up about "doing it right". EFT is very robust!

4 CONFIDENCE MADE EASY

- This book is designed to work by regular use **until you feel more confident in every situation.**

- You may prefer to set aside a day for doing it in one long session. Or you can plan one session of 60 - 90 minutes 1 - 3 days per week until you are done. Or whatever works for you.

- Typically clients go through this whole program within a minimum of six sessions. Sometimes lack of confidence has many facets and stubborn causes. If that is the case, simply persevere with this program, and you can get there, safely and gently.

- Do these exercises every day or every day that you can, until you are at the level of confidence that you desire.

- Having said this, please remember that some confidence fears are normal. For example, someone who lets go of a lack of confidence asking their boss for a rise may well go to their boss and confidently state the reasons why they deserve a rise and ask fot it; but not if they interrupt an important board meeting with the company's largest client and demand in a loud voice that they must get a rise! So you can rest assured that EFT will not make you act in a rude, selfish, or inconsiderate way. You can **simply let go of the unnecessary blocks in your path to confidence.** In other words, EFT can blast through the blocks in the way to becoming a more confident you!

- This may take a few sessions or it may take longer.

- Remember, **you are not in a race with anyone**. You only want results.

We often slip into old habits from time to time, and that is OK. If that happens, it just means that there is part of the fear energy still lurking around in your system somewhere. Be kind to yourself if this happens, use your book again till you are free from all of this lack of confidence.

If you have to miss some of the **acupressure points**, for instance because you may have eczema on one side of your face, that's OK.

If you are already an EFTer, you may wonder why I do not use the word "remaining" in my statements. Should you say "remaining" or "Even though I still have this remaining" as per the original EFT instruction? In my experience, the meaning of "remaining" changes with culture and language. Since I have an international clientèle, and this is an international book, I have deliberately left this out. I personally find it makes no difference. If you already use "remaining", please add it to the scripts here on all rounds after the first round.

This book is designed to simplify the tapping process so that you can have a ready-to-go personalized tapping script. The only thing that matters is that it works. If **it works for you, that is all that matters**.

You may find yourself experiencing a release of emotion through tears, laughter, giggles, burping, or coughing, If so, just **let it happen**, keep tapping silently on **any point** that feels right, it's **OK** to feel emotion. You have been suffering this stuck fear as an unknowingly suppressed bunch of negative emotions. Now you have made the decision to move on. Be kind to yourself. **Allow these negative emotions to surface, release, and leave your energy system.**

Make sure you have a glass of water nearby, and keep filling it up. It is ideal to drink water. EFT is thirsty work. You may find yourself breaking for the toilet, as the water has to go somewhere! That's perfectly normal. Occasionally, a **headache** is experienced. That is normal. It signifies the uncomfortable emotion is trying to leave your body through your head. You can tap for the headache too, tapping on all the points as you say "Even though I have this headache, I deeply love and accept myself". Sometimes it is a sign that you need to drink more water, as energy work like EFT needs a lot of water. You can also get up and have a stretch, and make sure you are in a comfortable, well-ventilated room.

5 COLLAPSING TABLE LEGS

With EFT, we bring up a little of the specific thing that bothers us and tap for it, then we bring up a little more and tap for that. And we carry on in this way till the whole thing has gone.

The best way to bring up this specific thing is to bring up an incident. An incident is a specific event. Even if this event has happened more times than we care to remember, we can remember one specific one. It may be the last one, or the first, or one that particularly jumps out at us. We can even make one up. This is because what your mind makes up is close enough to the truth to work with.

Experienced practitioners work on the concept of collapsing table legs.

Basically you have a table like that.

- The table has a table top. This is your problem, or issue.

- To collapse the table, you need to collapse the table legs, or what is supporting the table top.

- Usually, there are more than just the four legs shown here. And sometimes, there are many legs. But the concept remains the same. To collapse the table, you need to collapse the table legs, or what is supporting the table top.

- It is very good for a practitioner working with a client to find the main table legs holding up the table top. Then the table can be collapsed more quickly.

- Using a table as an example doesn't mean that we only have four table legs to collapse. It just helps explain how the process works

- With EFT, it is always good to find events to tap on. This makes the tapping specific.

- For the purposes of a simple illustration, these events are Event A, Event B, Event C, and Event D. In real life, there could be many more of these events, and on the very rare occasion, just one.

It is unimportant to break down all the feelings you have in this event. For instance, unless you feel you need to, there is no need to find out exactly how much anger, exactly how much fear, exactly how much sadness, and tap on each of them. The reason is that with EFT, **we tap on all the points in the meridian system that correspond to all the emotions.**

The EFT tapping procedure, even the popular shortcuts, include points for sadness, fear, anger, etc.

Every time you tap a round of EFT, you are tapping on special points in the meridian system that correspond to all these emotions.

This means that the tapping takes care of the sadness, the fear, the anger, etc. So we are free from the need to isolate the separate emotions.

This enables us to be extremely specific by honing in on a specific event.

So which table leg is the one supporting the table top?

There is a theory that whatever your mind brings up for healing is right. I agree with this. If in doubt, just tap on whatever specific event your (or your client's) mind offers.

It is important to stay focused on the goal here. EFT does not tap away specific events. It does not tap away root causes. It taps away an **energy disruption**. A common trap for tappers is to avoid tapping on what comes up for healing because the tapper deems the event not **"good enough"**. Or maybe the tapper deems that event "not core-issue". But **the mind is very powerful**. Your mind **will** come up with the right event for healing. Trust your mind. Use the tapping instructions to let go of what comes up. You can be pleasantly surprised how much progress you can make. All it takes is a little trust of what your mind is offering as an event.

6 PRELIMINARY PREPARATION

The tapping points given here are the recommended tapping points, in order to make tapping easy for anyone at any level of EFT experience.

This guide is designed to be fairly painless. On the rare occasion, there may be tears or discomfort. Should this happen, just tap silently on the Eye Brow, Side of Eye, Under Eye, Under Nose, Chin, Collarbone, Underarm, Karate Chop. Carry on tapping on all the points silently until the feeling subsides.

Confidence and self-esteem go together. It is easy to feel confident if you value yourself. And it is easy to feel more confident if you feel worthwhile.

Most of us start life feeling confident as a young fetus in the womb. Then one way or another, fear and doubt creeps in. Sometimes this starts out for reasons necessary to survival, then it just gets stuck as stuck energy. And sometimes this is because of the beliefs that we learn. Gary Craig calls these beliefs "The writing on our walls", and he does a wonderful explanation in The Palace of Possibilities DVD set. A negative belief is kept in the mind by stuck energy. Just like everything else in EFT, all you need to do is to somehow access the energy component and tap on it.   The nice thing about EFT is that you can notice a gradual change, as bit by bit, you are improving your confidence.

This program is written with the purpose of helping anyone with their confidence.

The Setup statements are to be repeated 3 times as usual. Except when there is more than one setup statement given; then you say each of them just once.

It is best to follow this guide from beginning to end. It is designed to be repeated from start to finish until you reach the desired level of confidence. It is like a lap of running, playing a piece of music, doing a circuit at the gym, playing a game of golf, or playing a computer game. Every time you go through roughly the same procedure, and your results improve with each time you play. In other words, repeat this book over and over again until you reach the desired level of confidence. Please treat this more like a process than an instant fix. This way, you have no excuse to beat yourself up if more issues come up for healing. Remember, **you are the person with the confidence to take this forward**. Enjoy it as if it is a game.

When you are ready, let's go to the next chapter and start EFTing for confidence! Just read-and-tap.

7   GENERAL TAPPING

This is designed to be used without SUDS or numbers. It is an important start to your tapping for confidence. It helps you ease into it. Just tap as follows.

Setup on Karate Chop:
I choose to be worthy of this tapping, and that's OK.
I choose to accept myself even when I can't, and that's OK too.
Just for today, I can accept myself a little bit more, including the part of me that lets me down. Just for today, that's OK.

Reminder on Top of Head, Eye Brow, Side of Eye, Under Eye, Under Nose, Chin, Collarbone, Underarm, Karate Chop:
I can accept myself a little bit more, just for today, and that's OK.

Setup on Karate Chop:
I allow myself to be worthy, and that's OK.
I allow myself to be confident, and that's OK.
I choose to be safely strong, and that's OK.

Reminder on Eye Brow, Side of Eye, Under Eye, Under Nose, Chin, Collarbone, Underarm, Karate Chop:
Safely confident and strong

Take a deep breath in through the nose, hold it, then slowly let it go through the nose... And let any remaining tension go... And when you are ready, just move on to the next section.

8 SELF-WORTH TAPPING

I suggest that you do this one particular chapter about once a week. You can do it on its own for about 10 minutes in the morning when you wake up, or during your lunch break. And then just forget about it for the rest of the day.

Some EFTers find this exercise so useful, they make it part of their daily routine. Whereas for others, it feels uncomfortable. Don't force yourself to do it if you find it too much. And if it really seems terrifying, you may choose to augment this book with practitioner sessions, so that you will be supported by someone else being there for you.

So, without further ado, this is how it goes:

How worthwhile do you feel?
50%? 20%? 80%? 2%? 40%?

Write this number down:_____

Now add 10% (or make the total 100%, as appropriate):
Your self worth + 10% = Your tapping number

For example, if you felt 20% worthwhile, add 10%, and that makes the total 30%. 30% Then becomes your tapping number.

Your tapping number is: _____

Tap the following tappings, filling in the blanks with your tapping number. Re-evaluate when the guide asks you to only. And you don't have to agree with the statements or believe them. just say them anyway. EFT works that way.

Trust me, I **know** you have challenges loving and accepting yourself. If it still feels too hard, just say instead
"I honour my feelings anyway".

So, tap as follows:

Setup on Karate Chop
I can be _____ worthwhile , and I respect, honor, forgive, and love myself.
Reminder on Top of Head, Eye Brow, Side of Eye, Under Eye, Under Nose, Chin, Collarbone, Underarm, Karate Chop
I can be _____ worthwhile.

(In this and subsequent tappings, if you feel 80-99% worthwhile, substitute "I am" for the "I can be". If "I can be" feels too overwhelming, substitute "maybe I can be")

Setup on Karate Chop
I can be _____ worthy of love, and I respect, honor, forgive, and love myself.
Reminder on Top of Head (TOH), Eye Brow (EB), Side of Eye (SE), Under Eye(UE), Under Nose(UN), Chin(Ch), Collarbone(CB), Underarm(UA), Karate Chop (KC)
I can be _____ worthy of love.

Setup on Karate Chop
I can be _____ worthy of acceptance, I accept myself with all my faults and failings.
Reminder on TOH, EB, SE, UE, UN, Ch, CB, UA, KC
I can be _____ worthy of acceptance.

Setup on Karate Chop
I can be _____ worthy of respect, I accept myself anyway.
Reminder on TOH, EB, SE, UE, UN, Ch, CB, UA, KC
I can be _____ worthy of respect.

Setup on Karate Chop
I am _____ worthy of good things, and that's OK.
Reminder on TOH, EB, SE, UE, UN, Ch, CB, UA, KC
I am _____ worthy of good things.

Do two rounds of this and re-evaluate your worthiness.

Write this number down: _____ Whatever the answer is, that's fine. **Even if it is the same number you have started with, that's fine too.** And now, on to the next section...

9 EVENTS TAPPING - TAPPING 1

Now we are ready to tap on events to reduce or eliminate their intensity. The easiest way to do this chronologically is to start with past events and finish with future events. The past events do not have to be in chronological order for the tapping to be effective. Start with this one so that you familiarize yourself with the procedure, and then you can proceed to any other tapping you choose.

Most of us have experienced some discomfort when they did a presentation or were at a meeting or social gathering. This often is related to early school experiences in some way, so I will choose this event to start with.

- Choose a time when you had to read out loud at school or perform in a school play or recital – or maybe at college or university.

Think of yourself looking at a DVD of this event in your hand. Just the DVD itself; the shiny disc. The DVD has the title of the film printed on it.

What would the title of the film be? Write it here:

My film's title is "_____"

- Take SUDS 10-0 or Small, Medium, or Large.
- Then tap, substituting your film's title in the gaps.

Setup on Karate Chop
Even though I have this _____ feeling, I accept myself anyway.
Reminder on TOH, EB, SE, UE, UN, Ch, CB, UA, KC
This _____ feeling.

For example, you can say something like this.

Setup:
Even though I have this feeling about the time when I had to read out in Miss Thomson's class, I accept myself anyway
Reminder:
The time when I was seven and had to read out loud in Miss Thomson's class

- Evaluate your SUDS or Small, Medium, or Large.
- Keep repeating the above tapping until you reach a SUDS of 2 or less or Small or less
- If it takes a few minutes or a few days of this tapping, that is OK. You are not in a race with anyone. Be kind to yourself and **go at a pace that is right for you.**

And next proceed to the next step.

This may be straight away after this or you may wish to start another time another day. Go at a pace that is right for you.

The rest of this page is blank to enable you to take a rest and decide whether to go further now or to put a marker at this point and come back to it the next time you are ready to proceed to the next step.

And now, when you are ready, proceed to the next step.

Imagine you now have the DVD playing on a black-and-white TV in front of you. On this DVD is this one particular incident when you felt you needed more confidence.

This film is a **very short film**. And we are looking at the **highlight of this film, its crescendo, the most intense moment**.

We are **not** dwelling on it. We are simply looking at it on a black and white TV in front of us.

Now **make it a still picture if you can**. Pause the DVD in your mind. This becomes a black and white picture.

- Take SUDS 10-0 or Small, Medium, or Large.
- Then tap, substituting your film's title in the gaps.

Setup on Karate Chop
Even though I have this _____ feeling, I accept myself anyway.
Reminder on TOH, EB, SE, UE, UN, Ch, CB, UA, KC
This _____ feeling.

For example, you can say something like this.

Setup:
Even though I have this feeling about when Mary giggled when I started reading, I accept myself anyway.
Reminder:
The time when I was Mary giggled when I started reading.

- Evaluate your SUDS or Small, Medium, or Large.
- Keep repeating the above tapping until you reach a SUDS of 2 or less or Small or less
- If it takes a few minutes or a few days of this tapping, that is OK. You are not in a race with anyone. Be kind to yourself and go at a pace that is right for you.

And next proceed to the next step.

This may be straight away after this or you may wish to start another time another day. Go at a pace that is right for you. The rest of this page is deliberately empty so that you don't rush ahead until you are ready. You may wish to bookmark it for later, or if you feel it is good to proceed, just go ahead to the next step.

In the next step, think of the film now as being shown on a color TV. Let the film run **quickly** to the end and get SUDS for the most intense moment.

- Take SUDS 10-0 or Small, Medium, or Large.
- Then tap, substituting your film's title in the gaps.

Setup on Karate Chop
Even though I have this _____ feeling, I accept myself anyway.
Reminder on TOH, EB, SE, UE, UN, Ch, CB, UA, KC
This _____ feeling.

- *Take your time, tap until you are done. Evaluate your SUDS or Small, Medium, or Large.*
- Keep repeating the above tapping until you reach a SUDS of 2 or less or Small or less
- *If it takes a few minutes or a few days of this tapping, that is OK. You are not in a race with anyone. Be kind to yourself and go at a pace that is right for you.*

And now, we are ready for the last part of this Event Tapping. As before, the rest of the page and the next are left deliberately empty. Proceed only when you feel totally comfortable to do so.

So, now proceed to the next step.

Close your eyes and imagine yourself there in the film. We are looking for emotions we didn't catch before. So really imagine the sounds, the smells, where you were standing, sitting, etc, and try to bring those feelings up.

- Take SUDS 10-0 or Small, Medium, or Large.
- Then tap, substituting your film's title in the gaps.

Setup on Karate Chop
Even though I have this _____ feeling, I accept myself anyway.
Reminder on TOH, EB, SE, UE, UN, Ch, CB, UA, KC
This _____ feeling.

- Take your time, tap until you are done. Evaluate your SUDS or Small, Medium, or Large.
- Keep repeating the above tapping until you reach a SUDS of 2 or less or Small or less
- If it takes a few minutes or a few days of this tapping, that is OK. You are not in a race with anyone. Be kind to yourself and go at a pace that is right for you.

Go through this exercise with different smallish events from childhood, as many times as you feel is needed. If only bigger events come up, then you can work with them anyway, but be very kind to yourself and make sure you take one step at a time. The nice thing about EFT is that you don't have to tap on all the unhappy events that happened to you. By only tapping on say 5-10 events, **the effect generalizes over most of the other similar events**. So, you do not waste time like being in therapy forever. You get done relatively quickly.

Should you feel uncomfortable during this or any other section, have a rest, and do the following calming meditation.

Lie down or sit back comfortably. Tap on both of your collarbone points with both hands at the same time. Keep tapping and:

- Breathe in through your nose
- Breathe out through your nose
- Carry on breathing in and out through your nose
- Take slower breaths in and out, take your time
- Notice your chest. Allow your chest to be still while your tummy appears to move slightly. This makes you breathe from your diaphragm and avoids hyper- ventilation.

- Allow yourself to take in small and slow breaths. This is your time, the whole world can wait. This is your time to relax, and that's OK.
- Keep tapping, taking small and slow breaths through your nose, and close your eyes for a few minutes.
- When you open your eyes again, allow a calm peacefulness to wash all over you, grounding you.

And next, when you are ready, proceed to the next step. Just tap as follows.

Setup on Karate Chop
I choose to be calmly strong, I accept myself.
Reminder on TOH, EB, SE, UE, UN, Ch, CB, UA, KC
Calmly strong.

Have a break. Maybe a day or so in-between this tapping and the next is good. It can help your energy settle. You can even wait a week. Or, if you are feeling up to it, you can just keep going. You choose. You **are** in control of the process, and that **is** OK.

10 EVENTS TAPPING - TAPPING 2

Find one specific event, a time when a parent was critical without meaning it, like "You may not be good at maths but..." Or "Your sister is prettier, but..." Or "You're brother is taller, but..." Or "You will never make it as an artist, you need a real job". By parent, I mean anyone in the position of parent. If your parents did not bring you up, then substitute for example a foster parent for parent.

If the parent never did this unkindness unless they meant it, you may wish to go easy on this one, take your time, and give yourself breathing space. **You do not have to tap on anything unless you want to**. And there is no need in being too proud to enlist the help of an EFT Practitioner to figuratively hold your hand during tapping on uncomfortable events. And cost need not be an issue. Many practitioners operate a sliding scale.

So, with this in mind, start with the following preparation.

Setup on Karate Chop
Even though this may be overwhelming, that's OK.
Even though there may be a resistance to feeling worthy, maybe I'm not used to feeling worthy, and maybe that's OK.
If at first feeling less worthy of criticism feels strange, of course everything new can feel strange, maybe I'll get used to feeling more worthwhile, and maybe that's OK.
Even if I feel guilty blaming [the parent] for this, I understand that I am not doing a blame exercise, I am simply releasing a block in my path to confidence, and that's OK.
Reminder on TOH, EB, SE, UE, UN, Ch, CB, UA, KC
This overwhelming feeling.

Repeat the above Setup and Reminder until you feel you can face EFTing the event.

Then write down the critical statement that your parent (or parent substitute said). You can write it here or on a piece of paper in front of you. If you cannot remember a specific one, make one up. EFT works well this way.

"   "
_____

- Simply look at the statement and take SUDS 10-0, or Small, Medium, or Large.
- Then tap as follows.

Setup on Karate Chop
Even though I have this feeling about this statement, that's OK.
Reminder on TOH, EB, SE, UE, UN, Ch, CB, UA, KC
This feeling about this statement.

Setup on Karate Chop
Even though I have this feeling about this statement, I am open to safely letting go of this feeling.
Reminder on TOH, EB, SE, UE, UN, Ch, CB, UA, KC
Safely letting go.

Setup on Karate Chop
Even though I have this feeling about this statement, maybe I can forgive myself and one day let go of the blame for others involved, for my own therapy.
Reminder on TOH, EB, SE, UE, UN, Ch, CB, UA, KC
This statement.

- Then tap as follows, substituting this critical statement in the gaps.

Setup on Karate Chop
Even though I have this feeling about " _____
_____* ", I honor my feelings anyway.*
Reminder on TOH, EB, SE, UE, UN, Ch, CB, UA, KC
"   "
_____

- Evaluate your SUDS or Small, Medium, or Large.
- Keep repeating the above tapping until you reach a SUDS of 2 or less or Small or less

And now proceed to the next step.

Close your eyes and imagine yourself there hearing the voice saying the statement. We are looking for emotions we didn't catch before. So really imagine the sounds, the smells, where you were, etc, and then open your eyes.

- Evaluate your SUDS 10-0, or Small, Medium, or Large.
- Then tap as follows.

Setup on Karate Chop
Even though I have this feeling about "_____
_____", I honor my feelings anyway.
Reminder on TOH, EB, SE, UE, UN, Ch, CB, UA, KC
"_____"

- Evaluate your SUDS 10-0, or Small, Medium, or Large.
- Keep repeating the above tapping, and then closing your eyes and imagining to evaluate the intensity of feeling, until you reach a SUDS of 0 or Small-or-less.
- Then tap as follows.

Setup on Karate Chop
I choose to be calmly strong, I accept myself. I accept myself even when I feel I can't.
Reminder on TOH, EB, SE, UE, UN, Ch, CB, UA, KC
Calmly strong.

OR you can choose to be the successful opposite of the criticism you heard, such as in the following example.

Let us say the critical statement was "You'll never make it as an artist"

The opposite of this can be "I enjoy the goodness of art" or "I choose to be a successful artist" or "I embrace artistic challenges" or "I allow abundance to flow for my art" or "I allow my artistic talent" or "I allow my talent to flourish"...

Then you tap as follows.

Setup on Karate Chop
I allow my talent to flourish, and that's OK.
Reminder on TOH, EB, SE, UE, UN, Ch, CB, UA, KC
I allow my talent to flourish.

Positive statements like this can be used as homework in-between sessions, tapping them between about 3 to 20 times a day to re-enforce the message.

Enjoy the healing journey.

When you are rested and ready for another session, you can then proceed to the next chapter.

11 EVENTS TAPPING - TAPPING 3

For this event, choose a time when you were bullied at school if this was the case. Otherwise, choose a time when a teacher, friend, boss, or colleague was over-critical.

Imagine a black and white picture of this event in front of you. if you cannot imagine it, just look at this one, it makes a good substitute.

If your picture had a title or caption, what would it be?

Write here the title of your (or this) picture:
" _____ "

Start with the following.

Setup on Karate Chop
Even though this may be overwhelming, I choose to be strong.
Reminder on TOH, EB, SE, UE, UN, Ch, CB, UA, KC
This overwhelming feeling.

Setup on Karate Chop
Even though this may be overwhelming, that's OK.
Even though others have treated me as if I was not worthy, Maybe I am a worthy person anyway, and maybe that's OK.
Even though some people are cowardly bullies, I no longer need to be their victim, I choose to be strong.
Reminder on TOH, EB, SE, UE, UN, Ch, CB, UA, KC
I choose to be strong.

Repeat the above Setups and Reminders until you feel you can face EFTing the event.

- Imagine looking at the picture of this event in black and white.
- Take SUDS 10-0, or Small, Medium, or Large.
- Then tap as follows, substituting your picture's title or caption in the gaps.

Setup on Karate Chop
Even though I have this feeling about "_____ _____", that's OK.
Reminder on TOH, EB, SE, UE, UN, Ch, CB, UA, KC
"_____"

- Evaluate your SUDS 10-0, or Small, Medium, or Large.
- Keep repeating the above tapping until you reach a SUDS of 0 or Small-or-less.

And now proceed to the next step when you are ready. Take your time, take it at your own pace.

Imagine this picture in color. Does it feel the same or worse? If it feels worse, simply repeat the tapping in the same way using the same statements until the intensity is 0 or Small-or-less.

Setup on Karate Chop
Even though this may be overwhelming, I choose to be strong.
Reminder on TOH, EB, SE, UE, UN, Ch, CB, UA, KC
This overwhelming feeling.

Setup on Karate Chop
Even though this may be overwhelming, that's OK.
Even though others have treated me as if I was not worthy, Maybe I am a worthy person anyway, and maybe that's OK.
Even though some people are cowardly bullies, I no longer need to be their victim, I choose to be strong.
Reminder on TOH, EB, SE, UE, UN, Ch, CB, UA, KC
I choose to be strong.

Repeat the above Setups and Reminders until you feel you can face EFTing the event.

- Imagine looking at the picture of this event in black and white.
- Take SUDS 10-0, or Small, Medium, or Large.
- Then tap as follows, substituting your picture's title or caption in the gaps.

Setup on Karate Chop
Even though I have this feeling about "_____ ", that's OK.
Reminder on TOH, EB, SE, UE, UN, Ch, CB, UA, KC
" _____ "

- Evaluate your SUDS 10-0, or Small, Medium, or Large.
- Keep repeating the above tapping until you reach a SUDS of 0 or Small-or-less.

Then proceed to the next step. The following page is deliberately empty for extra gentleness. Only proceed when you have finished this part.

Close your eyes and imagine yourself there actually in the event, as if it is happening. We are looking for emotions we didn't catch before. So really imagine the sounds, the smells, where you were in relation to the other person/people, etc, and then open your eyes.

- Evaluate your SUDS 10-0, or Small, Medium, or Large.
- Then tap as follows

Setup on Karate Chop
Even though I have this feeling about "_____
_____", *I choose to be strong.*
Reminder on TOH, EB, SE, UE, UN, Ch, CB, UA, KC
"_____"

- Evaluate your SUDS 10-0, or Small, Medium, or Large.
- Keep repeating the above tapping, and then closing your eyes and imagining to evaluate the intensity of feeling, until you reach a SUDS of 0 or Small-or-less.

And now proceed to the next step. Just tap as follows.

Setup on Karate Chop
I choose to be calmly worthwhile, I accept myself anyway.
Reminder on TOH, EB, SE, UE, UN, Ch, CB, UA, KC
Calmly worthwhile.

The rest of the page has been left empty to help you go at a more helpful and efficient pace.

One easy homework my clients like is something they can say to themselves throughout the day. Some choose to do it under the desk at work or in class. Others like doing it in their bedroom, or in the toilet. Some do it while watching TV or on a break. This is something you can do often.

Just tap on the Karate chop as you say your homework statements in your head three times. **If you are in a public place and do not want to be seen tapping, you can rub the Karate chop with your fingers instead of tapping it.** Practitioners may wish to write the statements on a small business-card sized card, so that it can be carried neatly in a wallet or purse.

Setup only on Karate Chop
I allow myself to let go of being a victim. I am a survivor. Just for today, I accept myself a little bit more. And that's OK, and I'm OK.

Tap the above statements about 3 to 20 times a day to re-enforce the message. It's *really easy!*

12 EVENTS TAPPING - TAPPING 4

For this event, choose a time when you were at a personal or business party or other gathering and needed more confidence.

Calm your mind and ask yourself:
"If this was a film on TV, at what point would you want to cover your eyes? In other words, at what point is that cringe-worthy moment?" Then ask yourself:

What would the title of the film be? Write it here:
My film's title is "_____"

It does not have to be complicated. For example, Mariam may have a confidence-lacking nervous-making memory of when she was at Dina's dinner party last Friday and Peter spoke to her. So her film's title would be:
"When I was at Dina's dinner party ;ast Friday and Peter spoke to me"

It really is that simple.

Then simply tap the following.

Setup on Karate Chop

Even though I don't like being judged, nobody does, I accept myself anyway.

Even though I am my own worst judge, I forgive myself, I love myself, I accept myself, even when I can't.

Even though I feel they are judging me, maybe by doing so I AM JUDGING THEM. Maybe I can accept myself anyway. Maybe I can forgive myself and anyone else involved in this.

Even though I worry about what to say, I choose to enjoy the quiet time in the conversation. I choose to use these breaks to gather my thoughts, have a rest, and that's OK.

Reminder on TOH, EB, SE, UE, UN, Ch, CB, UA, KC

I accept myself even when I can't.

Then proceed to the next step

1. Take SUDS 10-0 or Small, Medium, or Large.
2. Then tap, substituting your film's title in the gaps.
3. Re-evaluate intensity 10-0 or Small, Medium or Large,
4. If anything more than 0 or Small-or-less, repeat the following over and over again until you get 0 or Small-or-less.

Setup on Karate Chop

Even though I have this _____ feeling, I accept myself anyway.

Reminder on TOH, EB, SE, UE, UN, Ch, CB, UA, KC

This _____ feeling.

Some tappers get down to a zero in just one or two rounds of this, whilst others can take weeks of daily tapping for, say, half an hour at a time. That is OK. Just take your time and do this tapping until the incident is collapsed.

Then, when you are ready, proceed to the next step.

Close your eyes and imagine yourself there actually in the event, as if it is happening. We are looking for emotions we didn't catch before. So really imagine what was said, what was not said, what you were wearing, what the other people were doing, where you were sitting or standing, etc, and then open your eyes.

If you get any negative intensity, simply repeat Steps 1-4 above.

Close your eyes and re-evaluate again. If any intensity of emotion is felt, keep repeating Steps 1-4 above until you get a 0 or Small-or-less. Remember, everyone goes at their own pace. take your time and do this tapping until the incident is collapsed.

When you are done, have a break. Then when you are ready again, choose about 4 more events that you can tap on just like you did here.

The good news is that the effect of tapping on just a few events generalizes over all or most of them. So you only have to tap on a selection of events. Whichever ones your subconscious mind brings up for healing when you are ready are the right ones. Just go with the flow and allow the gentle release.

13 EVENTS TAPPING - BUSINESS

This script is designed to be repeated again and again until you reach the desired level of success. So if for example, you want help with presentations, in-person meetings and phone calls, you just repeat the script with each of these separate matters.

For this event, choose a time when you had to give a presentation or were at a meeting and needed confidence. Or maybe you are confident face-to-face but need help on the phone.

"If this was a film on TV, at what point would you really identify with the hero and wish you could help him/her? In other words, at what point is that moment where you feel you could have been stronger or more forceful?"

Then ask yourself:

Who was the presentation, meeting, or phone call with (client's name or colleagues)? This is then the title of your film. For example, if this was a meeting with Smith and Partners, the title of your film would be "Smith and Partners Meeting".

Write this down here:
My film's title is "_____"

Then simply tap the following.

Setup on Karate Chop

Even though I don't like the feeling of having to do it right, I choose to calmly and logically enjoy a challenge.

Even though I am my own worst judge, I like to do well, I criticize myself very well, a little too well sometimes. Maybe I can perform even better if I'm kind to myself, and maybe that's OK.

I choose to be calmly strong.

I CAN do this. Yes, I CAN.

Reminder on TOH, EB, SE, UE, UN, Ch, CB, UA, KC

I CAN do this. Yes, I CAN.

Then proceed to the next step

1. Take SUDS 10-0 or Small, Medium, or Large.
2. Then tap, substituting your film's title in the gaps.
3. Re-evaluate intensity 10-0 or Small, Medium or Large,
4. If anything more than 0 or Small-or-less, repeat step 2 until you get 0 or Small-or-less.

Setup on Karate Chop

Even though I have this _____ feeling, I accept myself anyway.

Reminder on TOH, EB, SE, UE, UN, Ch, CB, UA, KC

This _____ feeling.

Then, and only when the event seems to be collapsed in this manner, proceed to the next step. The next page is deliberately empty to help you go at a safe and effective pace.

Close your eyes and imagine yourself there actually in the event, as if it is happening. We are looking for blocks in your path that we didn't catch before. So really imagine what was said, what was not said, the body language, where you were sitting or standing, the lighting, the layout of the building, etc, and then open your eyes.

- Repeat Steps 1-4 above.
- Close your eyes and re-evaluate again. If any intensity of emotion is felt, keep repeating Steps 1-4 above until you get a 0 or Small-or-less.

Repeat with a few other business challenges, and then you will be ready to move on to the next step.

14 EVENTS TAPPING - FUTURE

For this event, choose a time in the future where you feel you need confidence.

This could be a business or personal event.

> Find one event, and give it a name. For example, it could be your 4-o'clock upcoming meeting, in which case, you can call it the "4 O'Clock Meeting". Or it could be a date tonight, in which case you can call it "Tonight's Date".

Write this down here:
My future event is called "_____"

Setup on Karate Chop
Even though I need to feel confident in this situation, I choose to be calmly strong.
Reminder on TOH, EB, SE, UE, UN, Ch, CB, UA, KC
Calmly strong.

Setup on Karate Chop
Even though part of me fears failure and another part of me fears success, I embrace all parts of me, and that's OK.
Reminder on TOH, EB, SE, UE, UN, Ch, CB, UA, KC
Failure, success, failure, success.

(experienced tappers can tap these alternate words on alternate points)

Then proceed to the next step

1. Take SUDS 10-0 or Small, Medium, or Large.
2. Then tap, substituting your future event's name in the gaps.
3. Re-evaluate intensity 10-0 or Small, Medium or Large,
4. If anything more than 0 or Small-or-less, repeat step 2 until you get 0 or Small-or-less.

Setup on Karate Chop
Even though I have this _____ feeling, I accept myself anyway.
Reminder on TOH, EB, SE, UE, UN, Ch, CB, UA, KC
This _____ feeling.

Then proceed to the next step. The following page is empty to help you go safely and effectively at your own pace.

Close your eyes and imagine yourself there actually in the event, as if it is happening. We are looking for blocks in your path that we didn't catch before. Then open your eyes, and if there is any intensity, proceed as follows.

- Repeat Steps 1-4 above.
- Close your eyes and re-evaluate again. If any intensity of emotion is felt, keep repeating Steps 1-4 above until you get a 0 or Small-or-less.

And now proceed to the next step. Just tap as follows, substituting your future event name in the gap.

Setup on Karate Chop
I choose to embrace challenges and go with the flow.
I am capable and strong.
I CAN do this. Yes, I CAN.
I allow an abundance of strength.
I allow an abundance of peace.
Whatever happens is fine. If anything really wonderful happens, that's a bonus. I allow this _____ to be OK, and I'm OK.
Reminder on TOH, EB, SE, UE, UN, Ch, CB, UA, KC
I allow this _____ to be OK, and I'm OK.

And that should be it!

15 EMERGENCY CONFIDENCE HELP

The treatments in this book involving future situations are very thorough. However, when you are actually in the situation itself, factors may arise that were not fully released as yet.

This is not because of anything wrong on your part
or the techniques used.

This is simply because we are only human, and it is not always possible to think of everything in advance.

Be kind to yourself. Although most will be fine in the previously challenging situation, if something does crop up, this chapter shows you how to handle it.

There are two emergency categories considered in this book:

1. A lack-of-confidence feeling when you are alone or with an accepting friend
2. A lack-of-confidence feeling when you are in public

If on your own or with an understanding friend or loved one, you can just do an emergency anxiety tapping. This **has no words and is easy to do** without having to think on the spot. If you need this in an **emergency**, tap quickly and silently on all these points for 5 minutes or as little or as long as you need, over and over again, in this order:

Under Eye
CollarBone
UnderArm
CollarBone

...

This is enough to calm the situation for most. Repeat if needed.

If in public, say on a train or plane or in a meeting, you may need to be more discreet. This book has so far included the main points used most commonly in EFT. I have deliberately left out the finger points for simplicity. However, if you know the finger points, they are excellent in an emergency. In the rare case where this is needed, you can rub your finger points, and **no-one will notice**. It's easy!

EFT finger points illustrated in blue/green on the side used

- The EFT finger points are on the side of the nail towards the top of the Thumb, Index Finger, Middle Finger, and Baby Finger.

- The ring finger is not normally used, as the point on that side of the ring finger is not as useful as the others. But it does not harm and can do good anyway. Do not fear it, you can easily use it. Some EFTers also use the ring finger, so you can include it for completeness.

- In a public place, you can simply rub these points as you say your EFT statement in your head. Use something simple, such as ¨Even though I´m really nervous, I accept myself anyway¨.

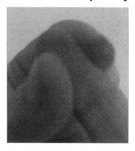

Rubbing a finger point

Just rub your finger points of one hand with the thumb and forefinger of the other hand.

- It doesn't matter which hand you use.
- Rub all these points silently
- Rub them over and over again for about 5 minutes
- Repeat if needed

Practice doing this now. It's discreet and easy!

And if you have gotten this far in the book without trying EFT at all, this is your cue to go back and get started. Get a pencil or pen to help you write your statements, so you can just do them with ease. Write down your intensity of fear and smile to yourself as you watch the numbers go down, down, and further down. Write down the new, lower intensities. Congratulate yourself for your healing efforts. Take it step by step. Tap yourself free.

16 AND FINALLY...

Thank you for buying this book

As always...

Wishing you peace and calm

ABOUT THE AUTHOR

Suzanne Zacharia is an experienced complementary health practitioner specializing in the mind-body-spirit connection. Suzanne started her therapy career as a result of getting miraculously better from serious illness through complementary care. Concentrating on her career full-time from 2002 as a hypnotist, Reiki healer and bodyworker, she soon discovered EFT and other kinesiology-based modalities, which completed the missing pieces of the puzzle.

Suzanne publishes her FREE EFT ezine at www.EFT-Scripts.com with free EFT suggestions for you to try (and a free EFT How-to for anyone who wants it). Suzanne also publishes a FREE record of her self-treatments with EFT. Prevention is better than cure, as they say, and this can be seen on www.blog.NewAgeLondon.com with many protocols people worldwide are referring to for improving their or a loved one's health. Emotional freedom and a positive outlook features strongly here, as the body can usually find a way to function well under many conditions, except when emotionally over-stretched.

Suzanne has two grown-up children in her native UK and lives in Cape Town with her spouse and cat.

Printed in Great Britain
by Amazon